FAVOURITE
HEREFORDSHIRE
and WYE VALLEY
RECIPES

compiled by
Dorothy Baldock

with illustrations
by A. R. Quinton

SALMON

Index

Cover pictures *front:* Ross-on-Wye from the Meadows
back: The River Wye at Hay-on-Wye
Title page: Monnow Mill, Monmouth

Printed and Published by J. Salmon Ltd., Sevenoaks, England © Copyright

Hereford Apple Dumplings

Apples, their centres filled with orange rind and currants enclosed in pastry.

12 oz. prepared shortcrust pastry	**Grated rind of half an orange**
4 teaspoons sugar	**1 dessertspoon marmalade**
4 cooking apples, peeled and cored	**¼ oz. butter, softened**
2 oz. sultanas	**Milk and sugar for glazing**

Set oven to 400°F or Mark 6. Roll out the pastry on a lightly floured surface and divide into 4 circles big enough to enclose the apples. Sprinkle each circle with a teaspoon of sugar and set an apple in the centre of each. Mix together the sultanas, orange rind, marmalade and butter and divide the mixture between the apples, filling the core hole. Bring the pastry up over the apples and seal firmly with a little water. Place the dumplings, upside-down, on a greased baking sheet and decorate the tops with any pastry trimmings, cut into leaves. Brush the dumplings with milk and sprinkle on a little sugar to glaze. Bake for 10 minutes, then reduce the oven temperature to 350°F or Mark 4 for a further 30 minutes or until the dumplings are golden brown. Serve with a little marmalade, warmed to make a sauce, or custard or cream. Serves 4.

Wye Baked Salmon

This pie was traditionally served on Good Friday, when meat was forbidden.
Originally the recipe also contained eels and oysters.

4 thick salmon steaks, wiped and trimmed   1 lb. prepared shortcrust pastry
1 small onion, peeled and finely chopped   3 oz. butter
2 oz. mushrooms, wiped and chopped   2 oz. fresh white breadcrumbs
Salt and black pepper   ¼ teaspoon ground cloves   ¼ teaspoon ground nutmeg
1 egg, beaten   Milk   2 tablespoons red wine   Juice of a lemon
Milk or beaten egg to glaze

Place salmon steaks in boiling water for 5 minutes, then remove the skin. Set oven to 350°F or Mark 4. Roll out pastry on a lightly floured surface using two-thirds to line a 2 pint pie dish, trimming the edges. Fry onions in half the butter until soft, stir in mushrooms and breadcrumbs and fry for 3 minutes. Remove from heat and add salt, pepper and spices. Stir in egg and enough milk to bind. Arrange salmon in the pie dish and spread on mushroom mixture. Melt rest of butter in a pan, add red wine and lemon juice and bring to the boil. Pour over the salmon. Roll out remaining pastry for a lid, sealing edges and trimming. Make a steam hole and decorate with trimmings. Brush with milk or beaten egg to glaze. Bake for 45 minutes or until pastry is golden brown. Serve with boiled potatoes and a green vegetable. Serves 4.

Bakestone Cakes

Rather more scones than cakes, these traditional Monmouthshire cakes
are cooked on a bakestone or griddle.

8 oz. flour	**½ oz. baking powder**
Pinch of salt	**2 oz. butter**

Single cream

In a bowl, sift together the flour, salt and baking powder, then rub in the butter until the mixture resembles fine breadcrumbs. Add sufficient cream to form a stiff paste. Roll out thinly on a lightly floured surface and cut into small rounds. Lightly grease a hot griddle or a heavy frying pan and cook, turning once, until golden brown. Split in half and serve hot, spread with plenty of butter.

Boiled Bacon and Cider Sauce

A traditional Herefordshire recipe.

**2 to 3 lb. bacon joint   Water   1 carrot, peeled and chopped into chunks
1 onion, peeled and quartered   1 bayleaf   6 peppercorns**
CIDER SAUCE
**½ pint dry cider   2 bayleaves   2 sprigs parsley
4 cloves   Pinch of dry mustard   Salt and black pepper
½ pint thick, well-flavoured brown gravy**

Place the bacon joint in a saucepan, cover with water and bring to the boil. Discard the water, add the remaining ingredients to the bacon joint and add sufficient fresh water to cover. Bring to the boil, then simmer gently, allowing 20 minutes to the lb. plus 20 minutes over. Drain the bacon well. Remove the rind and serve hot with boiled potatoes, carrots and celery and accompanied by the cider sauce.

CIDER SAUCE: place the cider, herbs, spices and seasoning in a saucepan, bring to the boil and simmer until reduced approximately by half. Stir in the gravy, bring to the boil and simmer, stirring from time to time, until reduced approximately by one third. Strain into a sauceboat and serve with the boiled bacon. Serves 4 to 6.

Kerne Bridge, River Wye

Spinster's Cake

This Victorian, or earlier, farmhouse fruit cake probably takes its name
from the unmarried daughters or sisters who acted as family housekeepers.

¾ lb. flour   Pinch of salt   1 level teaspoon bicarbonate of soda
4 oz. butter   8 oz. sugar   8 oz. currants   4 oz. raisins   2 oz. flaked almonds
1 oz. candied orange and lemon peel, chopped
½ oz. caraway seeds   ½ teaspoon ground ginger   ½ teaspoon mixed spice
Approximately ½ pint buttermilk

Set oven to 375°F or Mark 5. Sift together in a bowl the flour, salt and bicarbonate of soda, then rub in the butter until the mixture resembles fine breadcrumbs. Stir in the remaining dry ingredients, then add sufficient buttermilk to form a fairly soft consistency. Turn into a greased and base-lined 8 inch round cake tin and smooth the top. Bake for 15 minutes, then reduce the oven temperature to 350°F or Mark 4 and bake for a further 1½ to 2 hours, covering the top with a piece of kitchen foil if it appears to be browning too quickly. Test with a skewer and when cooked, cool in the tin for 5 minutes, then turn out on to a wire rack.

Winter Vegetable Soup

This warming farmhouse soup can be made from a variety of vegetables,
but leeks and potatoes always predominate.

3 large potatoes, peeled   3 large leeks, washed and trimmed
1 onion, peeled   2 carrots, peeled   2 sticks celery, wiped and trimmed
½ small turnip, peeled   ½ small swede, peeled   1 to 1½ oz. butter
1 oz. flour   2½ to 3 pints chicken or vegetable stock
Salt and black pepper   A bouquet garni
Fresh chopped parsley for garnish

Dice the vegetables. Melt the butter in a saucepan, add the vegetables, cover and sweat over a low heat for 5 to 10 minutes. Remove the cover and stir in the flour, then pour in the stock, stirring all the time. Add the seasoning and herbs. Bring to the boil then simmer, covered, for 40 to 50 minutes. Remove the herbs and serve, garnished with parsley and accompanied by crusty bread. If preferred, this soup can be liquidised, enriched with milk or single cream and served garnished with a swirl of cream and chopped parsley. Serves 4.

Hereford Brandy Snaps

Originally known as 'jumbles' or 'gaufers', meaning wafers, brandy snaps were traditionally sold at fairs. These were a particular feature at the Hereford May Fair.

3 oz. butter	4 oz. flour
4 oz. sugar	½ teaspoon ground ginger
4 oz. black treacle	1 teaspoon brandy
1 teaspoon lemon juice	

Melt the butter, sugar and black treacle together in a saucepan and leave to get cold. Set oven to 350°F or Mark 4. Stir the flour, ginger, brandy and lemon juice into the treacle mixture and combine very well. Drop teaspoons of the mixture on to a well-greased baking sheet and bake for 10 minutes until golden. Allow to cool slightly, then roll each one round the well-buttered handle of a wooden spoon to form 'rolls' before they set. The easiest way to do this is to bake the brandy snaps in very small batches. Allow to cool completely and serve either plain or filled with whipped cream flavoured with brandy.

Monmouth Stew

Lamb has always been a popular ingredient for stews and casseroles and this one contains leeks and pearl barley. If desired, this stew can be cooked, covered, on top of the stove.

1½ lb. stewing lamb, cubed or 8 lamb chops, trimmed
1 oz. seasoned flour   1 oz. butter or oil
4 to 6 leeks, washed, trimmed and cut into rings   2 oz. pearl barley
4 sprigs of parsley, 1 sprig of thyme and a bay leaf,
tied together with a piece of kitchen string
Salt and black pepper   ¾ to 1 pint lamb stock

Set oven to 350°F or Mark 4. Coat the lamb in the seasoned flour, heat the butter or oil and lightly fry all over for 1 minute. Add the leeks and fry for a further minute, then transfer to a casserole dish. Add the pearl barley, herbs and seasoning, then pour over the stock. Cover, bring to the boil and cook gently for 1½ to 2 hours. Remove the herbs before serving and serve with boiled potatoes. Serves 4.

Honey Cake

*Honey has traditionally been a popular sweetener,
giving a faintly gingery flavour. This is a Herefordshire recipe.*

**8 fl. oz. clear honey   3 oz. butter   12 oz. flour
1 teaspoon baking powder   Pinch of salt   1 teaspoon cinnamon
1 teaspoon bicarbonate of soda   3 oz. chopped mixed peel
3 eggs   3 tablespoons milk   Grated rind of a lemon
1 oz. flaked almonds (optional)   3 tablespoons clear honey**

Set oven to 325°F or Mark 3. Place the 8 fl. oz. of honey with the butter in a saucepan and heat gently until melted, stirring continuously. Sift the flour, baking powder, salt, cinnamon and bicarbonate of soda together, then stir in the peel. Beat the eggs and milk together and stir into the honey mixture with the lemon rind. Make a well in the centre of the dry ingredients and add the honey mixture gradually, beating well between each addition. Turn the mixture into a greased and lined 8 inch square cake tin and sprinkle with the almonds, if desired. Bake for 1 to 1¼ hours until the cake is firm, yet springy to the touch. Using a fine skewer, prick the surface of the hot cake and pour on the 3 tablespoons of honey. Cook in the tin for a further 10 minutes, then turn out on to a wire rack.

The Wyndcliff near Chepstow

Spiced Apple Cheese

Fruit 'cheeses' and 'butters', a classic country way of using up gluts of fruit, would be potted in straight-sided jars. They improve with keeping – sometimes for more than a year – and this recipe was traditionally served at Christmas, with hazelnuts and whipped cream.

3 lb. windfall apples, washed and quartered, but not cored or peeled
8 to 10 cloves and a good ½ inch piece of cinnamon stick, tied in a muslin bag
Approximately ¼ pint cider or water
Preserving sugar   A small 'walnut' butter, optional

Place the apples and spices in a preserving pan and pour over the cider or water (there should be sufficient just to cover the apples). Bring to the boil, then simmer, stirring from time to time, until very soft. Remove the spices and rub the apples through a sieve. Measure the resulting pulp and allow ¾ lb. of preserving sugar to each 1 lb. of pulp. Place the pulp and sugar in a clean preserving pan over a gentle heat and stir until all the sugar has dissolved. Then boil gently, stirring regularly to prevent sticking, until the 'cheese' is sufficiently thick so that when a wooden spoon is drawn through it, it leaves a clear line. ('Butter' is boiled to the consistency of thick cream.) Remove from the heat and stir in the 'walnut' of butter, if desired. Pot into clean, warm jars, cover, label and store in a cool, dark place.

Butter Tarts

Popular throughout Monmouthshire and Wales,
these delicious tartlets are a traditional teatime treat.

8 oz. prepared shortcrust pastry	**1 egg, beaten**
3 oz. butter	**A few drops vanilla essence**
6 oz. soft brown sugar	**2 tablespoons single cream**
4 oz. raisins or sultanas	**A little milk, optional**

Set oven to 350°F or Mark 4. Roll out the pastry on a lightly floured surface and use to line 12 to 16 lightly greased tartlet tins. Melt the butter in a saucepan, stir in the remaining ingredients and spoon into the pastry cases, brushing the pastry edges with a little milk, if desired. Bake for 20 to 25 minutes or until golden. Remove from the tins and cool on a wire rack.

A.R.QUIN

Midsummer Pudding & Cider Sauce

This steamed suet pudding usually has a filling of redcurrants and raspberries, but in Herefordshire, dark blue whortleberries – also known as bilberries or blaeberries – and black crowberries were preferred. As these may now be unavailable, blueberries can be substituted. Midsummer Pudding is traditionally served with cider sauce.

**8 oz. prepared suet pastry   1½ lb. prepared fruit – redcurrants, raspberries etc.
4 oz. sugar to taste   1 scant dessertspoon water containing a squeeze of lemon juice**

CIDER SAUCE
1 pint cider   ¼ lb. sugar   2 to 3 oz. butter

Roll out the pastry on a lightly floured surface and use three-quarters to line a buttered 1½ to 2 pint pudding basin. Add half the fruit, sprinkle over the sugar, then add the remaining fruit and spoon over the water with lemon juice. Roll out the remaining pastry to form a lid and place on the pudding, wetting and sealing the edges well. Cover with buttered greaseproof paper and seal with kitchen foil. Steam over a saucepan of boiling water for 1½ to 2 hours. Serve with cider sauce, custard or cream. Serves 4 to 6.

CIDER SAUCE: simmer the cider and sugar together to form a light syrup, stirring from time to time. Cut the butter into small pieces and whisk into the mixture. Pour into a sauceboat and serve at once.

Love in Disguise

A Herefordshire dish that was popular in the 18th century.

4 prepared hearts, calf or lamb
¼ to ½ lb. forcemeat stuffing of your choice
8 to 10 rashers streaky bacon, rinds removed and slightly stretched
4 oz. vermicelli   2 oz. fresh white breadcrumbs
1 egg, beaten   A little lard or butter, melted

Set oven to 350°F or Mark 4. Stuff hearts with the forcemeat stuffing (amount will depend on size of the hearts) and sew up. Wrap each heart in bacon rashers, securing with wooden cocktail sticks. Wrap each in lightly buttered foil, place in a baking tin and bake for 1 to 1½ hours. Break vermicelli into small pieces, place in a pan of lightly salted water and boil until tender. Drain well, allow to cool, then mix with breadcrumbs. Remove hearts from oven, discard foil and allow to cool slightly. Brush thoroughly with beaten egg, then coat with vermicelli mixture, pressing it on well. Sprinkle the hearts with melted lard or butter. Grease baking tin, place in hearts, and bake for 20 to 30 minutes, until coating is crisp and golden brown. Carefully remove sticks and serve with creamed potatoes, a green vegetable and a rich gravy. Serves 4.

Duck in Honey and Thyme Sauce

An elegant country house dinner party dish from Herefordshire.

2 oz. butter   4 prepared duck breasts, cut in half
3 shallots, peeled and finely chopped   5 tablespoons white wine
2 oz. honey   Juice of half a small lemon
4 sprigs thyme, ideally lemon thyme   A curl of lemon rind
Salt and black pepper   ½ pint double cream
Thyme sprigs and lemon garnish slices for garnish

Melt the butter in a skillet and lightly fry the duck pieces on both sides. Add the shallots and cook until soft. Carefully remove the duck pieces and keep warm. Strain off any excess fat. Add the wine to the shallots and bring to the boil, stirring, then add the honey and lemon juice. Stir until the honey has dissolved, then add the thyme, lemon rind and seasoning. Stir in the cream and heat through thoroughly. Return the duck pieces to the skillet, cover and simmer very gently for 15 minutes or until tender. Place the duck pieces on a warm serving dish. Remove the thyme sprigs and lemon rind from the sauce and spoon over the duck pieces. Serve garnished with thyme and lemon slices and accompanied by minted new potatoes and green peas. Serves 4.

Welsh Cinnamon Cake

*Dark in colour and almost 'gingery' in flavour, this is one of the
most traditional cakes to be found in Monmouthshire and Wales.
It rises little during cooking and its texture resembles rather spongy shortbread.*

4 oz. butter	**½ lb. flour**
4 oz. sugar	**½ teaspoon baking powder**
2 egg yolks	**1 teaspoon ground cinnamon**
	1 tablespoon apricot jam

Set oven to 400°F or Mark 6. Cream the butter and sugar together in a bowl until light and fluffy, then beat in the egg yolks, a little at a time. Sift the flour, baking powder and cinnamon together and stir into the egg mixture. Knead to a soft dough, then roll out on a lightly floured surface. Fit into a buttered 8 inch round cake tin with a removable base and bake for 25 minutes. Place the cake on a wire rack and while still hot, brush over with warmed apricot jam. After brushing with jam, the cake can be topped with meringue, using the spare egg whites, then baked for a further 10 to 15 minutes at 350°F or Mark 4 until the topping is golden.

Monnow Bridge, Monmouth

Potato Pie

This supper dish found in both Monmouthshire and the Welsh counties,
is traditionally served with pickled beetroot or pickled red cabbage.

2 lb. potatoes, peeled and cut into quarters
¼ pint milk   1 oz. butter
4 oz. grated cheese, strong Cheddar or similar
Salt and white pepper
2 to 3 oz. white breadcrumbs, lightly crisped
A little melted butter

Boil the potatoes in salted water until cooked. Set oven to 400°F or Mark 7. Drain the potatoes well, add the milk and butter and mash until smooth, then stir in the cheese and seasoning. Butter a 1½ to 2 pint pie dish and sprinkle with the breadcrumbs, pressing them to the base and sides with the back of a spoon. Spoon in the potato and cheese mixture and rough up the top with a fork. Brush with melted butter and bake for 20 to 30 minutes or until golden brown. Serve with pickled beetroot or red cabbage or with crusty brown bread. Serves 4 to 6.

Oat Cakes

Served plain as 'teatime biscuits' as well as with cheese, country housewives would use up stale oatcakes by crumbling them into buttermilk to make a porridge for breakfast or supper. The addition of flour makes the oatmeal dough easier to handle.

6 oz. fine or medium oatmeal   2 oz. flour
½ teaspoon salt   Pinch bicarbonate of soda
1 to 1½ teaspoons sugar, optional
1 tablespoon melted lard or bacon fat
2 to 3 teaspoons melted butter   Hot water
1 egg beaten with 1 tablespoon of milk or water and
1 teaspoon sugar (optional) to form a glaze

Mix together in a bowl the oatmeal, flour, salt and bicarbonate of soda, then add the sugar, if desired, melted fat and sufficient hot water to form a stiff dough. Knead lightly, then divide into balls. Place a thin layer of oatmeal on a board and either roll out the balls or shape with the hands, into thin rounds, about 2½ to 3 inches in diameter. Place on a greased and preheated griddle or heavy frying pan and cook gently until the underside is dry and the edges begin to curl. Glaze the top just before the end of cooking, then remove and cool on a wire rack. Traditionally stored in piles, these oatcakes will keep in an airtight tin for several weeks.

Beef Olives

*Originally known as 'Beef aloes', this is a very old dish
that became particularly popular in the 17th century.*

1 to 1½ lb. steak, cut into thin slices	**1 bayleaf**
4 oz. forcemeat stuffing of your choice	**Salt and black pepper**
1 oz. lard or 1½ tablespoons oil	**1 tablespoon red wine, optional**
2 onions, peeled and sliced	**Cornflour**
1 pint beef stock	**1 or 2 bayleaves for garnish**

Stretch the steak slices gently, then divide the forcemeat between them. Roll up
and secure with fine kitchen string. Heat the fat or oil in a skillet and fry the
onion until golden, then add the 'olives' and brown lightly. Add the stock,
bayleaf and seasoning, bring to the boil, cover and simmer gently for ¾ to
1 hour or until the meat is tender. Lift out the 'olives' with a draining spoon,
remove the string, place on a heated serving dish and keep warm. Add the red
wine, if desired, to the liquid in the pan and heat through. Remove the bayleaf,
thicken if necessary with a little cornflour and pour over the olives. Serve,
garnished with bayleaves and accompanied by creamed potatoes, carrots and a
green vegetable. Serves 4 to 6.

Salt Duck

This recipe appeared in 'The First Principles of Good Cookery', published in 1867. The book was compiled by Lady Llanover, who lived for much of her life in Monmouthshire and had an enormous enthusiasm for all things Welsh. Salt Duck has a very fresh taste and is usually served with onion or laver and orange sauce, laver being a form of edible seaweed.

**1 large fresh, prepared duck, approximately 3½ to 4 lb. in weight,
purchased two days before required
6 oz. sea salt**

Wipe the duck, then rub, inside and out with a quarter of the salt. Place on a large dish in refrigerator. Later, repeat process with a further quarter of the salt, turning duck in any brine that has formed. The following day, repeat process twice, using up remainder of salt. Next day, when duck is due to be cooked, wash thoroughly, inside and out, under cold running water to remove all traces of salt. Set oven to 350°F or Mark 4. Pat duck dry with kitchen paper, place in a casserole dish and just cover with water. Cover casserole, place in pan of simmering water and cook for 1½ hours. Remove duck from casserole, drain *very* well, and place in a baking tin. Increase oven to 450°F or Mark 8 and roast duck for 20 to 30 minutes until skin is crisp and golden. Serve with spinach and onion or laver and orange sauce. Serves 4.

Tintern Abbey from the South West

Buttered Apples

In Herefordshire, this quickly made farmhouse pudding is usually served with cider sauce.

1 lb. cooking apples, weighed after peeling and coring

6 oz. sugar   6 oz. butter   3 thick slices stale bread, crusts removed and cut into cubes

A little extra sugar, optional

CIDER SAUCE
1 pint cider   ¼ lb. sugar   2 to 3 oz. butter

Cut the apples into slices and roll in the sugar until completely coated. Melt half the butter in a frying pan and fry the apples until golden brown and soft. Keep warm on a serving dish. Melt the remaining butter and fry the bread cubes until golden brown and crisp. Lightly combine with the apples, sprinkle over a little extra sugar, if desired and serve at once, accompanied by hot cider sauce or whipped cream. Serves 4 to 6.

CIDER SAUCE: Simmer the cider and sugar together, to form a light syrup, stirring from time to time. Cut the butter into small pieces and whisk into the mixture. Pour into a sauceboat and serve at once.

Sultana Cake

A simple Herefordshire farmhouse fruit cake.

6 oz. butter	Pinch of salt
6 oz. caster sugar	4 oz. sultanas
3 eggs	1½ oz. mixed peel
10 oz. flour	1½ oz. glacé cherries, quartered
1 teaspoon baking powder	Grated rind of half a lemon
	Milk

Set oven to 350°F or Mark 4. In a bowl, beat the butter and sugar together until light and fluffy, then add the eggs separately, beating well between each addition. Sift together the flour, baking powder and salt and stir into the mixture, then add the sultanas, peel, glacé cherries and lemon rind, combining well. Add sufficient milk to make a fairly stiff mixture and turn into a well-greased and base-lined 7 inch cake tin. Smooth the top and bake for 1½ hours or until the cake is golden brown, covering with a piece of kitchen foil if it appears to be browning too quickly. Cool in the tin for 5 minutes then turn out on to a wire rack.

Trout with Herbs and Cider

*Noted for its cider-making, cider is a popular ingredient
in both savoury and sweet dishes in Herefordshire.*

4 prepared trout   1 oz. seasoned flour   1½ to 2 oz. butter
2 tablespoons fresh, finely chopped mixed herbs – parsley, thyme, basil etc.
Juice of half a lemon   4 tablespoons dry cider
2 to 3 tablespoons single cream   Lemon slices and sprigs of herbs for garnish

Cut each trout into two fillets and coat in seasoned flour. Melt the butter in a
frying pan and stir in the herbs. Add the trout fillets and fry for 3 to 5 minues,
turning once. Add the lemon juice and cider, cover and simmer over a very low
heat for a further 3 to 5 minutes. Carefully remove the trout fillets, place on a
heated serving dish and keep warm, then stir the cream into the cider mixture
and heat through. Pour over the trout fillets and serve garnished with lemon
slices and herb sprigs and accompanied by boiled potatoes. Serves 4.

Monmouth Pudding

In Victorian times, bread-based puddings, such as this, were considered ideal fare for children and adults with delicate digestions. Monmouth Pudding has a light, soufflé-like texture, and when served reveals bold red and white stripes.

8 oz. fresh white breadcrumbs	**2 oz. butter, melted**
½ pint milk	**3 egg whites**
¼ teaspoon vanilla essence	**Red jam – raspberry, strawberry, etc.**
2 oz. sugar	**A little sifted icing sugar**

Place the breadcrumbs in a bowl, bring the milk to the boil, pour over the breadcrumbs and allow to soak for 10 minutes. Set oven to 325°F or Mark 3. Stir through the breadcrumb mixture with a fork to break up any lumps, then add the vanilla, sugar and melted butter. Whisk the egg whites until they stand up in peaks and fold into the mixture. Spoon a thick layer of jam over the base of a buttered 1 to 1½ pint soufflé dish and cover with half the breadcrumb mixture. Add another layer of jam, then top with the remaining breadcrumb mixture. Bake for 30 to 40 minutes and serve at once, dusted with a little sifted icing sugar. Serves 4 to 6.

Marmalade Teabread

A moist, spicy cake traditionally served as part of a high tea meal in Herefordshire.

7 oz. flour   1 teaspoon baking powder
1 teaspoon ground ginger (optional)   2 oz. butter
2 oz. soft light brown sugar   4 tablespoons orange marmalade
1 egg, beaten   3 tablespoons milk
1 oz. candied orange peel, finely chopped (optional)

Set oven to 325°F or Mark 3. Grease and base line a 1 lb. loaf tin. In a bowl, sift together the flour, baking powder and ginger (if desired), then rub in the butter until the mixture resembles fine breadcrumbs. Stir in the sugar. Mix together the marmalade and the beaten egg and stir into the mixture, then add the milk and mix to form a soft dough. Turn into the prepared tin and smooth the top, pressing on the orange peel, if desired. Bake for 1 to 1¾ hours until golden brown, covering the top with a piece of kitchen foil if it appears to be browning too quickly. Allow to cool in the tin for 5 minutes, then turn out on to a wire rack. Serve sliced, plain or spread with butter.

Symonds Yat, River Wye

A R QUINTON

Frazzled Beef

Sometimes known as 'Frizzled Beef', this quickly-prepared Monday wash day meal, used up Sunday dinner leftovers. Originally the fat used in this recipe would have been beef dripping.

A 'walnut' of butter or a little olive oil
1 or 2 medium onions, peeled and finely chopped
Cold mashed potato   Salt and black pepper
8 slices cold roast beef

Heat the butter or oil in a frying pan and fry the onion until soft. Stir in the potato, season well, press down to form a 'pancake' and cook on both sides until golden brown. Remove from the pan on to a heated serving dish and keep warm. Add a little extra butter or oil to the pan and lightly fry the beef slices on both sides to heat them through. Arrange on top of the 'pancake' and serve with a thick brown gravy. Serves 4.

Salmon in Cider

The salmon is baked with shallots and basted with cider. The cider 'cuts' the rich oiliness of the salmon; if desired, claret can be used as a substitute.

2 to 3 lb. middle cut salmon cleaned and washed
1½ oz. butter   Salt and black pepper
½ teaspoon ground nutmeg   2 small shallots, peeled and chopped
1 dessertspoon fresh chopped parsley   2½ to 3 fl. oz. dry cider

Set oven to 375°F or Mark 5. Cut the salmon into 4 equal slices and arrange in a well-buttered ovenproof dish. Season with salt, pepper and nutmeg. Mix together the shallots and parsley and sprinkle over the salmon. Dot with butter, then pour on the cider. Bake for 15 to 20 minutes, basting frequently. Serve with buttered, boiled potatoes and with tomato sauce, to which a little of the strained cooking liquid has been added. Serves 4.

Hereford Cider Cake

A cake traditionally served at harvest suppers.

4 oz. butter   4 oz. caster sugar   2 eggs
8 oz. flour   Pinch of salt   1 teaspoon ground nutmeg
¼ teaspoon ground ginger   A scant half teaspoon bicarbonate of soda
5 fl. oz. cider

Set oven to 375°F or Mark 5. In a bowl, beat the butter and sugar together until light and fluffy, then add the eggs one at a time, beating well between each addition. Sift together the flour, salt, spices and bicarbonate of soda. Whisk the cider to make it slightly frothy, then fold it into the mixture, alternatively with the dry ingredients. Combine well together and turn the mixture into a well-greased and base-lined 7 to 8 inch square cake tin. Smooth the top and bake for 50 to 60 minutes or until the cake is golden brown and springy to the touch. Allow to cool in the tin for 5 minutes, then turn out on to a wire rack. Store the cake in an airtight tin for one day before cutting. Though it is not traditional, 2 oz. sultanas that have been soaked in 2 tablespoons of cider overnight, can be added to the mixture.

A.R.Qu

Stuffed Pork in Cider Sauce

A Herefordshire farmhouse recipe.

1 to 1½ lb. pork tenderloin, cut in half lengthwise
2 oz. butter   1 large onion, peeled and chopped
2 rashers streaky bacon, derinded and chopped
1 large apple, peeled, cored and chopped
2 oz. breadcrumbs   1 tablespoon fresh chopped parsley
1 teaspoon fresh chopped sage   Salt and black pepper
1 egg, beaten   1 tablespoon flour   ½ pint dry cider

Flatten the two pieces of tenderloin slightly. Melt the butter and fry the onion until soft, then add the bacon and apple and fry for 1 to 2 minutes. Stir into the breadcrumbs in a bowl, add the herbs and seasoning and bind with the beaten egg. Spread the filling over one half of the tenderloin, top with the other half and tie in three or four places with kitchen string to keep its shape during roasting. Set oven to 350°F or Mark 4. Place in a roasting tin with a little oil and roast for 1 hour, basting occasionally. Remove from the tin, cut off the string, place on a heated serving dish and keep warm. Stir the flour into the juices in the tin, add the cider and bring to the boil, stirring. Serve the tenderloin with the sauce poured over, accompanied by creamed potatoes, mushrooms and grilled tomatoes. Serves 4.

METRIC CONVERSIONS

The weights, measures and oven temperatures used in the preceding recipes can be easily converted to their metric equivalents. The conversions listed below are only approximate, having been rounded up or down as may be appropriate.

Weights

Avoirdupois	Metric
1 oz.	just under 30 grams
4 oz. (¼ lb.)	app. 115 grams
8 oz. (½ lb.)	app. 230 grams
1 lb.	454 grams

Liquid Measures

Imperial	Metric
1 tablespoon (liquid only)	20 millilitres
1 fl. oz.	app. 30 millilitres
1 gill (¼ pt.)	app. 145 millilitres
½ pt.	app. 285 millilitres
1 pt.	app. 570 millilitres
1 qt.	app. 1.140 litres

Oven Temperatures

	°Fahrenheit	Gas Mark	°Celsius
Slow	300	2	150
	325	3	170
Moderate	350	4	180
	375	5	190
	400	6	200
Hot	425	7	220
	450	8	230
	475	9	240

Flour as specified in these recipes refers to plain flour unless otherwise described.